D1200664

Cobras

by Colleen Sexton

BELLWETHER MEDIA • MINNEAPOLIS, MN

Cobras are **poisonous** snakes with narrow bodies. Most cobras are 4 to 6 feet (1 to 2 meters) long.

The king cobra is the largest poisonous snake in the world. It grows as long as 18 feet (5.5 meters)!

Cobras come in many colors. They can be yellow, brown, or black. Some cobras are pink, cream-colored, or red-brown.

Large spots, small dots, and dark bands often make patterns on their skin.

Cobras have three layers of skin. **Scales** make up the inner layers. The outer layer is dry and smooth.

Cobras grow throughout their lives. They must **shed** their outer skin whenever it gets too tight for their bodies.

= areas where cobras live

Cobras live in Africa and parts of Asia. There are about 20 kinds of cobras in the world.

Cobras are found in many **habitats**. Some live in rain forests. Some live on mountains.

Other cobras **slither** through grasslands or across dry deserts.

Some live near water or spend all their time in trees. Cobras even live in large cities.

Cobras are **predators**. They hunt frogs, snakes, lizards, birds, rats, and other **prey**.

Cobras bite their prey with sharp, curved **fangs**. The fangs are hollow. A poison called **venom** flows through the fangs and into a bite.

The venom **paralyzes** animals. They stop breathing and die. Cobras then swallow the prey whole!

Some animals hunt cobras. Eagles and **mongooses** are fast hunters. They can catch and kill cobras without being bitten.

mongoose

Cobras hiss and raise the front of their bodies off the ground when they are in danger.

They spread bones near their heads to make a wide **hood** of skin. The hood makes a cobra look big.

hood

Some cobras have spots on their hoods that look like large eyes. The spots can fool predators and let cobras get away.

Some cobras can spit venom
at predators. They can blind their
predators and then escape!

Glossary

fangs—sharp, curved teeth; cobras have hollow fangs through which venom can move into a bite.

habitat—the natural surroundings in which an animal lives

hood—skin near the head that is stretched wide; cobras open their hoods when they are in danger.

mongoose—a slender, furry animal that is known for killing cobras and other poisonous snakes

paralyze—to make an animal unable to move

poisonous—able to kill or harm with a poison; the venom that a cobra makes is a poison.

predator—an animal that hunts other animals for food

prey—an animal hunted by another animal for food

scales—small plates of skin that cover and protect a snake's body

shed—to let something fall off; snakes rub their bodies against rocks or trees to help shed their skin.

slither—to slide

venom—a poison that some snakes make; cobra venom is deadly.

To Learn More

AT THE LIBRARY

Fiedler, Julie. *Cobras.* New York, N.Y.: PowerKids Press, 2008.

Gibbons, Gail. *Snakes.* New York, N.Y.: Holiday House, 2007.

Gunzi, Christiane. *The Best Book of Snakes.* New York, N.Y.: Kingfisher, 2003.

ON THE WEB

Learning more about cobras is as easy as 1, 2, 3.

1. Go to www.factsurfer.com.

2. Enter "cobras" into the search box.

3. Click the "Surf" button and you will see a list of related Web sites.

With factsurfer.com, finding more information is just a click away.

Index

The images in this book are reproduced through the courtesy of: Ron Kimball/Kimballstock, front cover; Heuclin Daniel, pp. 4-5; Tony Phelps/naturepl.com, pp. 5 (small), 13 (small); Thomas Lozinski, p. 6; D. Fernandez & M. Peck, p. 7; Bildagentur Waldhaeusl, pp. 8-9; McDonald Wildlife Photog./Animals Animals – Earth Scenes, p. 9 (small); Jon Eppard, p. 10 (small); Minden Pictures, pp. 10-11; M. Watson/ardea.com, pp. 12-13; Juan Martinez, p. 14; Lynn M. Stone/naturepl.com, p. 15; Mary McDonald/naturepl.com, pp. 16-17; Pascal Goetgheluck/ardea.com, p. 17 (small); photolibrary, p. 18; EcoPrint, p. 19; Rick Strange/Alamy, p. 20; Omar Ariff Kamarul Ariffin, p. 21.